The Thankless Paths to Freedom

The
Thankless
Paths to
Freedom

Wake Forest University Press

Medbh
McGuckian

First North American edition
First published in Ireland in November 2022 by
The Gallery Press and edited by Peter Fallon
Poems © Medbh McGuckian, 2024
For permission, write to
Wake Forest University Press
Post Office Box 7333
Winston-Salem, NC 27109
wfupress.wfu.edu
wfupress@wfu.edu
ISBN 978-1-943667-12-3 (paperback)
LCCN 2024931940
Design by Crisis
Publication of this book was generously
supported by the Boyle Family Fund.

Contents

for Anne Devlin
and Carol Tweedale Bardon

The content of freedom is revealed by two basic manifestations in Europe—first, life in polarity: Europe itself has developed the counter position for every position.

Europe is Europe perhaps only because it is capable of becoming everything.

—Karl Jaspers, 'The European spirit'

Two European phenomena are rooted in freedom—consciousness of history and the will to knowledge. At the centre of European man, dominating the great moments of his life, there lies an essential absurdity.

—André Malraux

The perforated silver of a bird-bone.

The Thankless Paths to Freedom

Colour Mistakes

Well before they reached London
they both knew they had passed
the pitch of their loving. Again the house,
the cloud deck, average weather, keeping
his back to the window behind his desk,
he assembled the terminal documents
he had collected with so much effort
over the previous months, odd numbers
of *The Humanist Quarterly*.
I didn't know how light and dangerous the rope,
the world jammed with unshed roses, rosettes,
is that area of white in my bedroom mine?
A word is missing here, he feels the word subside
in a right-hand tremor, since spirit is never
transparent to itself, or another doubling
of meaning is taking place here. Time's hand
touching, after time has flown, hangs the dated
death by a blue heavenly, a reckless
blossoming, like the vine sponge to the highest eye.
Soothing fictions—the real change is less
in the city than in himself. His book was not about
the world but about itself. His wantonness
was the appropriate response to such a chaotic

place. The bell lips hoping to climb to fame
on your coat-tails. The work will flower and he die,
under his single European sky, the empty spaces
in his story ready to face the next downturn,
the new thin foreseeable routes, a long-breathed
melody like a long, prolonged, and repeated kiss.
The map of most of the sky is stale,
a long strip would blow the star apart,
stray radiation from the newly dead
exits a tunnel to find itself back
at its entrance. A river cannot, we are told,
rise above its source. I feel your radio-quiet
pulse among your hard drive's nested folders,
wrapping our heads around copies of this book,
of you and me. The silver poisoned sky
mistakes your colour as a soundless event,
a victory garden where snow is replaced
by gloom. The shroud pin is staining Virgin
Mary in a dress with triple-dot motif
and, just as he reworked it, so it fell apart.

Without a wedding, the dim flame of the lilac
brushes the sense of many houses, stretching
all around, though the prison smell is absent.

He's sleeping, he's full, of the slowest possible
blood, until the last trumpet, to kiss it into him
all over again, that rainless summer.

But she's faithful to the one who took her first,
with wings of thickened air, beside the red
and orange garden, where the trees are immune.

His book, he said, must be like linen, in answer
to some kind of bouquet, only here the light
is looking at your January 1st letter.

On Sundays she is in church but not visible
as she sings in the choir. She already believed
the letters of her new handwriting, there is a heavy *K*.

I'll soil it with cherries. When we 'go out' along
the boulevards coloured snowflakes circle
your maroon eyes with white, like tears of protection.

The epidemic's impact seems to have been major,
the parting above Mary's brow lay quiet,
garnished with thick clouds that looked like shapes of water.

The year 1921 ends on page 100 and the wind
is a completely new character among the mingled
flowers, wide channel for all my rivers.

The poetry addressed to you is swarming over me,
the way she backed into marriage, shopping
in the often empty stores for margarine and loganberry jam.

The Hotel Picardie

Slack-jawed, floridly unwell,
I disassembled the television
in my reverie-plus and swallowed
the contents over twelve hours' sleep
without repair, pounding hemp.

I awoke to find myself filled
with time, every mark was another
small victory for the clock.
There was no touch from the peephole
that punctuates the door.

The not-yet-events lose
their lustre: you need to wade
to unhook from the past,
from the specialist winter-over syndrome.
There were more parts than I began with.

Mrs Much-wed

The obedient plant, known as summer snow,
with close-set spikes, lanterns when closed,
stars when open, laps the terrace walls,
plunges down to woodland in its hollow.

A dim woman, cloistered in ill health,
she was engaged with the wholesale slaughter
of adjectives, to stir up a violent stench
in the language, her radiance never sleeps.

She cried a lot, tore up handkerchiefs,
just sleep and sleep, for here's the switch,
I like a bed like a swimming pool myself.
Is it your idea I should be your Organ City?

Why shouldn't a virgin want to stretch
and turn over, now and then? In which
of these rooms did she not sleep, while
all the while I was playing the quiet friend,

the poetess with the boiling brains,
with one light high inside? A ripple
of flame all over me muffled the words
in a little blur of silk.

She puts her thin white lips to my heart,
lips just far enough apart for the reflection
of the upper one to deepen the colour
of the other. As if an angel had gone about

lifting gravestones, the gravestone by the far gate
seems more articulate than the living.
As the moon-track seems to draw
a boat across the water.

A stage wind always whistling
through sea with its everlasting
shuddering and sighing. Kissed
by him, she sits as if folded in wings.

A halt of her husband ahead,
useless legs, one so oddly protruding.
Why was she on her knees, crouching
instead of lying flat on her stomach?

With a slight drag of one foot,
woman, what have I to do with thee?
That a person should have to lock themselves
into their clothes in a trusting mood after sex.

Her gratitude to God whom she did not
believe in, like a T-shirt with no message on it.
Her eyebrows now very scanty,
the cheapest box, into the ground immediately.

One longs to go to a hospital and have something
cut out; the whole church is lined with heartbeats,
it isn't cathedral enough. We seem to be
driving through the landscape of a missal

or a when-valley-was-in-flower book.
Lawns as brown as doormats, burning
and being burnt, other semi-tender
shrubs, perfume of hemlock woods.

Rooms and their reasons, in an honest
house, as sad a room as the shut-up best
parlour. The lamps have found
a clever way of coming together,

peach-bloom porcelain, directly in front
of you, the heart-shaped hooks,
the willow armchair, mother-of-pearl
buttons for the servants' bells.

On a day not fashioned for me a masked physician
left handprints on my upper thighs.
I held a pose on tiptoe throughout the razor blade
raised to my cheek, the sound bleed's unseen
drumming.

Advent was proceeding and gardens gradually left
for the forests of thy. The west wind's mercy
was still in heat, silver trickled along the shore
of the farm beneath the sand,
rain saddened the boats.

I suffered my heartbeat in its bodycomb,
that closet of dark scrapbooks where your mouse bones
spread under the earth, your fingers of wood
feather the roof to a tall edge,
you assemble, fold again,

your fractions of eternity like lunar fires.
The willows in their year-round green
weep properly, consider February as another
salt-white cover for the soft dust
leaked from the drained bed.

When the attunement we call 'a body' ends,
in the sparest of signs, this nothing else
is spreading across the thinning membrane
of our most interior simmering
to pulse it into 'light' later on.

The Feather Shop

Although the country is loveless
they are gently setting roads
into the landscape, passive houses,
room for the river.

The building fine-tunes its facades
as when one blows on a flower
or birdhearts so proudly frigid
lines on a daughter path.

My notebook was like my garden,
iris garden, storm-water garden.
It holds, slows and cleans water
to a nearly vivid streak.

When she stood trial at the loosening fair,
recently widowed, penniless,
drunk, for the theft of six
pewter plates and an iron bedscrew,

I saw her pull two out of her bosom,
her Damascene moment, her sacrament money,
her elopement from the house and infamous
behaviour, unlawfully begotten on her body.

My mother's head had been bad from the night
of the thunder, whose innings of dreamings are done.

The first of every month I don't be right in my mind
since my daughter had that child in the garden.

It was dark when she was delivered of her infant,
Winter, they began to wash the stairs with water

from boiled foxglove, lungs that would float
until the pleasure of the Lord Lieutenant.

The sky of poetry is big with child again too,
God help me. My humble attempt at blank verse

was laudanum-inspired 'Lines to Him Who Will Understand
Them', largely improvised on the spot.

That sauntering drab of slender reputation, the fair
authoress, Brilliana Mildmay, with roots in the provinces,

has her tender sonnets reproduced on creamware,
and a string of celebratory dinners; they bought up

the whole of the first printing in a day. Herself
fills the foreground, her concubinage to share

the Sapphic throne, the peculiar
suggestive red of the walls.

I have found that books
are of the least use when most wanted.

                                    By the by,

I have been at the play, walking in so well
in a dress that will blush in the dark,
I whirled through the whole round
of impertinence, being forced to ask
every morning what victory there is
in a froth sort of thing, unclean orchids.

I have seen the whole opera house
turn to look at her arm and hand
on the front of the box, at the single
patch to the side of her upper lip.
Of myself there is nothing left
but an eyebrow window
in the sky garden: my soundcloud what
a bee might hear in a hive, my sapphire
needle what the moth believes.

I am flounced into diagrams of generals,
how many phone minutes till the *Carpathia*
responded, the Morris Room where seasons

fall from eye level into warm
grey on the floor.

Maybe it is the hardest place to be,
opening myself up yet again, forbidden
even from clenching my fists. I cannot
hardcore with my wraps, belts and chalk:
my coat of muscles is a shell to be polished.
Feel my arms, at my peak I would be considered
just bored. My pin-up posters flare
like stained-glass windows, I medicate
for the early nights, eight years down the line.

The Plume Trade

We shave an hour off our sleep
while the longer winged birds
take a scene from the north
and apply it to the south's

too constant light, too south.
I let the moon shine in my eyes,
the right hand mock moon, till
all meaningless days are eyelids coming down.

Like a cloud we are pushed
from all directions, beneath the weight
of winter, your summer self, sash of roses
a simple brown that the story voice tells.

Sarah was putting on her hoops,
Lourdes gave birth in her hammock.
Somehow their hands and dresses
overlap, my knee a desk, sisterbook.

When I was in my right mind
my body was doing its best without me—
when I say 'talking of myself'
I mean there are two of me.

They walked breast to breast,
never touching, at crocus time,
in Bally I forget what, it is
on the coast, open to gunboats.

Each child dropped on to the plot
a bunch of spring flowers,
fleurettes of novembrance, secret
mourning full of rememberers.

Our shrouds were already as cold
as the wounded trains, as houses
that grow on top of houses, as understorey plants
that begin to leaf out, from the thongs of self.

The comma butterfly drains the light,
blue after rain like the more everyday
sort of angel. Dewy one, angelic one,
golden you, strange and unkind birth.

She plaits her hair into the growing seaweed,
that fiery abundance refusing to turn grey,
organic diamonds faithing the brown thorn.
Her swaddled flesh is labelled Elegy.

The name lay heavily in the air, silence
concerning silence. I lavished all my gifts
on ungrateful sleep, until the last
darkness or moments just before she arrives

and, inevitably, she wakes. Can you
the strange snows endure of his most frigid
poetry, can you on delicate feet
settled frost support, the myth hedges?

The deep green price of language is not
to slash mindlessly at spiders' webs,
the nature of the unwisdom, the unbinder,
the undoer, the uncreator, the much-shelled

omnipresent but useless church.
A daughterless woman, with lustrous flecks
on her lips, huge tiger-scratches.
Where her car had been parked was

a large crater where ideals are
might-have-beens.
Arise, mind, from the low unwilling
site of the quenched funeral.

Nine Types of Solitude

A single sky-blue bomber
disappears like a pulse with a growing
completeness, to geoengineer
a sunshade, seed the stratosphere
with interbraided black swans.

Raw steam from the angriest ocean
whispers the turmoil down
into the spent fuel pool, the bone bed.
Birds of precious feather measure
the weather of the unoccupied zone

where the dead think with superhuman
speed, and the child of one life
becomes the brother of the next.
Two lives, as it were, are not enough.
You're not twenty, don't burn like this.

With families re-peopled by imposters
and books in corners greying into nothings.
Daymares and word salads, my Mary's
breastplate had a different quilting point.
She tore her back, belladonna and bromide.

Her cheek is marked with a golden bell
whose sound can wash through windows
like a ghostly bell from the past
with dew on its tail, like the sermon bell
very light from morning rain that saw

the day off. No more than one short
peal, when any is passing out of life
into the technology of salvation
where time is forever starting over again
and the pain is greatest, earliest.

Angels are sophisticated machines,
not alive, not people who go freely
to unravel into silence. Everyone complains
of the time of too late, of the lack of news,
though there has never been so much

as a cloud's response. I stare
at the unpolluted sky all night,
night-wedded to the Lord of the Near,
to find something worth saying
about the lyrical halo of illness.

Sometimes just the movement of a pen
across paper is the most ununderstandable
carbon-addicted doorstep to all houses'
voices, almost as if one had crept in
while the owners had gone out for a moment.

A Wineskin in the Frost

The floor, if there is one, is a space
of black words giving out their scent.
The way before the way before
is a word as common as bitterness.

Like a garden tightening its grip
the string of her loins threatened to snap,
bracing her shaking legs and burning knees,
her swollen, dusky-red feet.

Remember you must leaf the dark-fanged
rose through the lid of the room when sorrow
curdles your foxglove cheeks and the window
behaviour of the field ends with a river.

Suddenly I am to have no innerness
any more: on Holy Saturday I enter
the rosary. I open it, set it in motion
till it is closed. Everything that is started

has to be closed, especially the stillness
of the rosary, that something was left
without a proper answer. I was born
in the rosary, time is a rosary,

each person is a bead; if one suffers
we suffer too. The chain of belonging
has no obvious pulse but to live and act
the power of the chant, the power of the number 3.

Not everlook, not ever look, at the raising
of the most important flagpole, but others'
hands, one another's mutual perceivings
upturning the dark to sleep upon a mirror,

since no one knows what the past will be
made of next (snow dying in the lake,
a hood laid on the mountain). I have to
find my body in his movements

weighted in places that had no real weight
in them. Propelled out of the sensation
by concepts that did not bend around me,
walking the length of the field and back.

His body amplifies my hips and the surface
of my body which is feminine, as if the motion
were happening to, rather than emerging from,
the body. Undulations from the feet

cycle up to the torso; I turn into a gentle
wave, dissolving away from life
into someone else. My momentum
was pruned, and the only way I could

achieve an intentional fall was
to become plural, to reassemble, to reform
my own colouring each dawn,
and haunt myself, seeking an outlet.

Star Patient

The winter silks are beautiful
as blossoms falling from a supernatural
curtain. The curve of streets
in growth-giving shadows
is like a jewel box tormenting
the altar steps.

Roofs half-dreaming in light
reach over leaves in wind;
they are blown into things,
things are blown into them.
Houses mindlessly set
in a reborn city of sparkle to me.

Winter believes that space.
They kept pouring a forest
into the scooped out coffin
with its fine Colmcille face:
plum and grey, honey and brown,
to alter the fabric of the body,

and so of whatever clouds,
knowledge, every cloud wedded

to the air, to the garden of your mouth.
Why travel to nature, we fold them
into the world we inhabit,
into rivers dry at their mouth.

Thin clouds stretch late gold
and impossible blue. The cool
sharp fog sprays words
and a hollow between words
over the evening floor of the brain
till night devours the road

and the Irish sun reels
like the inside of a slit
envelope into the aimless new
morning. The mountain
of my father rises at hip
and shoulder, you never know

which father. My neck swings,
pulling my black wings
over my shoulders, my head tips
on the top of my spine.
I beg my mind to stay
the same seventeen thoughts,

a metal chair. It unfolds
into a stretcher with an arm-shaped

heaviness. I can feel the bedsprings
in my back, twisting upwards,
screwing me into the bed.
The sea has dropped.

Other people think I have
a glass back. I want my bones
back, a flower like a firework
the colour of rust. If a saint,
she remained invisible,
the semi-plena white rose.

Bethlehem Candle, £70

O Come let Him adore you.

These greys of the weather I write out prescriptions,
the diagnosis of the diagnosis.
In the mildewing house I use a white sage
smouldering smudge to cleanse the rooms.

The offensive stained-glass windows
were icing my wrists at night. I began mostly
living in my car, rich with place, imagining
how far these graves have travelled.

The sky is hung in a semi-circle, the din
of our single frozen bone-dry moon
being dragged across by wires measures
the dimming of the star nearest the sun.

The stairs at the end of the corridor became
an open knife, the streets are portrayed
as if running about trying to find out
what happened to the placehood of planets,

the old land of violent stars that bathe
their companions in x-rays. The cathedral steps

solidify in the sting of a fine rain,
and the life-size burnt Christ offers

a salvation of sorts, the drawing of a reverse
namaste. His tongue can move in prayer
and death appears as smooth, irregular
and latticelike, with deep skyscraper roots.

I resolved not to add echo;
I also attended Spirit's funeral
which spent its first winter on Mars;
they live there on Mars time,

commanding it to take one last picture,
a view of Mars's sedate mossy yellow alleyways,
tea-colour wing-flap under water,
shading the water, rustling like a mouse

below snow. The man who drove the getaway car
into the old landfill site that is due
to be turned into a park made a flood-grey
bruise in the sky the size of a thousand Hiroshimas

to widen her, the high quality juice
with the comforting scent of roses,
the angels of questions, angels with answers,
the three angels you bought last Christmas.

Removing the Martian Sky

Yes, Mars is darker since we switched off Spirit.
Spirit's third winter feeling out the rock
on Mars was her last. I know this and still
go searching for some trace of love's infolding.

One way of reading white is all it takes
not to buy anything else. Sometimes, when the moon
is young, birds fly to the moon for the winter
and become moon clues, our chemical cousins.

So there is less and less sweetness in the quieter
countries (in which the story pauses a little),
the darker, thinner birds blacken the sky,
their washed away nests soft bark under twigs.

With little or no honeysuckle, all flowers
are knocked to the ground, in forest patches
months ago, when autumn came, damp pearl
essence of the blue lily, as winter deepens.

The Elsewhere Empire

In a glint of red candles and throat pleats
the house feels composed. White chrysanthemum
revolution. The starling's black bill turns yellow
in the spring, fake bird of paradise.

I had you living beside me, a young saint,
glorious cub of the household. I invented
a sister for you, named Paula, her possible soul,
our eternal possessions, our digital perpetuity.

Sometimes our concern with moonrise,
its insistence on midsummer and midwinter,
is like a detail of a burial of any unsettled souls
in a sea of electrified language, dashes of lime

on the wall itself. The smoke-grey coat
of a laceworks of death—*mavrone*, for me,
there is no after the war, the rain of an earlier day,
the balmy elsewhere of winglets past the flowers

in their rifles. The diet was so poor, men's voices
did not break till they were twenty, not really believing
what they knew. And every time I turn on an electric
light I believe that love, The Orchid Hotel, South Flower St.

While she was rooted to her bed along braided
pathways I saw an advertisement that the mountain
was for sale, frost wedging extra virginity
woven around the dark nutmeg seed.

She is buried with herbs of love, ghost fishing.
The sound of one's footsteps start to fade,
the stairs feel as if they descend further than they do,
or feel like a room in themselves, an afterthought.

The Bidding Prayers

1. AFTER THERMIDOR

First raindrops in the air are being torn,
a huge distance softened it, out there
the stars. The shots are dry and always
doubled, the lost and almost dead bullets
within the beautiful silence of the grass,
within the warscape.

The war had never ended, or had not
ended for us, surely I have been sixteen
years asleep, in sheets woven
from the eyelids of doves. In the middle
of a pre-election season we are like
the shipbuilding industry, in a permanent
state of reconversion.

We were leaning more towards the Dead Kennedys,
where are you, damned? We can't wait for streets
or slow-turning vehicles on to the roadbed,
the ribbon sidewalks. Streets can change
between the poem-cards, let's go that we're leaving,
one downcast afternoon.

2. JEWEL SONG

I must lose you again and cannot,
the other other. Of what direction
was my ardour, a breath away from my eyes,
eyes that have skins as mists before them,
the optic yield of the day flapping loose
all around, from the morning windows.

I bewailed the drowsiness of my converse,
my inner goddess feelings of lowered consequence.
I'd grown aware of some new flimsiness
in my body, of voices muffled through
wood and plaster. Let the nostalgics know
that this is their month.

I wear a cherry hat, a sister's worth of grey,
and I, now Marchioness of Newcastle, in petal-
flecked shoes, such tainted linguistic scraps.
The smell of damp flags in the sleepy
bi-national city humours herbs into a balm,
the grand-sounding word 'redeeming'

soothes leaves among the thoughtful horses,
like verses for women who cry 'Apples',
like the beamless nature of dreams
and other mental disorders. Like mathematics
and other matters of the heart. Someone
cupped my breasts in the plum-coloured dust.

My head feels full of powder and black pins,
the art of ingeniously tormenting. I make
the path in hypersleep, my distemper for the flowing
of flowers drenched by the steel medicine
and the occasional angel in her cybersleep pod.
Very unblue, she lived as happy as two angels

joined as two worlds at the end of their Poles
for whom death is a kind of rhyming. Dressing
is the poetry of women, sapphire stockings
with a metal thread, mossy black stars on her cheeks.
When words were things that came to pass
she is Duchess of Newcastle now.

Little can be said about the apricot frost
that added white to the darling harbour,
the weather we meet and the different
ways in which it rains—the rain in the poem

wasn't falling. They were tearing out
the middle lane of the beltway near
our home while the slightest deviation
from the conduct expected of her

was caught in loops of thinking,
in that image thought gives itself
of what it means to think, or dream
through the internal clouds coming to

in the muscled heart. Unabated
haunting in the daylight by extreme
close-ups of her mouth crumpling up
in the withdrawal of her lips

brightened the curtains with initial
light-enhancing waters. Small reflections
shine on books. We taste the accumulated
silence of the fierce, drab, absurd,

streets of Belfast's
one vast clinic.
We fall prey to hope
in limited sun.

Kepler 452b

Numbers are useless in counting anything
like perfumed rosaries made of plumstones
knotted in the shape of a rose. There is only
one universe at a time; the one real world
earlier on, when we were simpler than we are
now, is soaked through and through with time.

The roses spelled out one word—partner—
any flashier miracle in the unsunned snow
or the blur of summer. I remembered how
the irises' skill in clearing up after themselves
was like shadow children against a secluded
gate, blue snowflakes, first fat drops of thunder.

I should re-insert the moon into the narrative
of the war. In fact I felt like a bonfire,
full of dull smoke, as if I were treading
the rim of a wheel burning a string
of crudely knotted flags. Dried blood on several
hundred candles fluttered towards the street.

Dark as those nights may have been, as the ghosts
of pens long dead, I sat and swayed

in my drowsy conflagration, kicking the tight-
laced city moodily behind me, step by step,
yet not advancing an inch. The streaks
of the sun furled up on the curtain, the brightness temperature.

As if my hand had been a skinless heart
or a raw telescope for tours of the afterlife,
sudden frosting moonmilk on a semi-infinite
cloud, starless cores surrounding a young star.
The stale preserved breath of the dead
who once ruled a world that now seems of no

importance hooded the streetlamps,
the church bells throbbing in the towers,
guarding forgotten dumps in abandoned bases
and empty petrol tins that shuffled like claws
to possess the half empty town. I saw much
of these scarecrow troops, the way their youth was humbled,

bled grey with boredom. Young soldiers everywhere,
standing about in shut streets on rainy Sundays,
on midnight platforms where no trains came.
They whistled and wished to be anywhere
but here. There were times when there seemed
to be no one else but these in the city,

city of expired fanaticisms and cold, closed
lamps. Soldiers, priests and beggars, sleek

black priests stepping like cats on a petal
as though to extinguish a match, while the afternoon
sun sucked up the flavour of each cramped
tree, surely the most painless way to be wakened.

Their Christ was carved from old wood
the colour of moonlight, lilies tied to his feet,
his toes already stirring, like the weight
of the leaves on the trees. The children were
especially quiet, my notebook was snatched
from my hand, they didn't like the look of it,

sniffed at, shaken, thumped hard, held upside
down. I was pretending to be a ghost,
my face stroked by the lighthouse
with its own grey roof of weather, and every scrap
of old cloth run up on a pole. I had ridden
wrapped up in a Union Jack to protect me

from the sun and, when I rolled out of it,
I felt that I was born. Or feeling well for once,
here and there, beginning with a window
and a streak of wind letting in the sky,
drawn by some need every evening to look
out to sea, not knowing what my prayer should be.

Abusers of the flag have no arm to cling to.
I had to wrestle with just such an angel,

stout angel in black dress, not an agreeable saint,
the whole poise of the evening. Not long ago
we exited a century, like prisoners of a language
learned against our will—now every thing breathes 2018.

As if the body needs to re-think the river
of the world-otherwise story before it
comes home. It is not certain that a bee
in his tapestries can hear this honey-
centred hum with his flight muscles
brushing it away like a bell for sleep.

The Unanxious One

It seems she killed an officer point blank.

The unintended beauty of this map
of bomb damage crosses lines
with the names of the winds. Brown
mountains rise in chains and brackish lakes
reveal the river's past, its dark tints.

Cherubs look through a telescope
from outside the sky, through a layer
of different coloured stars, or flown
stars, bits of a star gone wrong, placing
weapons there, the wreckage from retired satellites.

Master of sleep, she gave me her limp hand
and returned to the oiling of her automatic,
her revolver, which she kissed affectionately,
then a rude crucifix made of black metal
till a lip of metal formed beads on her forehead.

Leaflets of green paper with black edging
remoulded the breast of the menstruating moon,
dark even in India. Blind flowers scorched

the quaint psyche knot at the crown of her hair
at the price of cutting Ireland in two.

The lake's moodswings and its tame listless saints
put me in thinking of a field of kinland I once owned
and its seven different names, its heaping up of stones.
It was free draining and could be ploughed dry
even after a deluge.

Spring has come with great difficulty.
We stood whole days in a cloud of water
since the first days of winter moved in.
He is half-dust already.

It was deep into April, the city
was soft as a palace of flowers
or linden honey. We would have stopped
the beating of our hearts if we could.

In a room with a real floor the powers
that were spoke for what one might call
the Provisional wing. They inhabit
an island, and long ago have shed and unlearned

all native marks and notes. Anything
alphabetic has a pastness about it
ab ovo, though we delight in a visitable
past, as if the flags meant nothing.

When the train began to move
I closed my eyes. It did not stop
at any station, but ran on as if
it had lost its mind, ran to the side,

then turned and rolled into
an open field. So it played
its lamp, the disorder
of drinking it in deeply,

such a smoky gem, whether
it should be prised free.
Mary Antrim, the name means
receptacle in Italian, tub or vat,

but also edge or border,
flower border, edge of page.
I was as kind to her that evening
as I knew how to be,

her head bloodied by a stone.
I filled a bowl with berry juice
for darkening her shawl,
that mystic, chemical change,

as one who has gone over to Rome
in attempt to make existence
shockproof. Other leaves in the story
are Lamb House, where single lady

penfriends hang yearningly
about a locked door—
so thickly besieged a shrine—
the devoted elderly widow

with her inexhaustible
collection of relics. He became
supersubtle, deciding to work
the garden: but why should he not

slink past in immortality,
in the figured tapestry,
the long arras that hides him,
while the good season lasts?

It is now, always, the bloodless past,
the wounded present, so unlike the groomed
groves that do not mind being swept
away. Every third thought that flounders
in me is dressed in a mist, with a train
of blue and black moths.

These grandfathered byways are unchanged
as ghosts are, thatching made of wings
of white birds, wattling of silver.
The translation of the white is rather
the white of flowers that are conditioned,
perfected by the camber of a wing.

Fields of dreamflowers unnoticed by
the dream me—why do I feel that the
seven roses require some explanation,
some further readjustment, some continuation
of the story? So that eyes may gradually
become fortified by unvisited gardens.

I have occasional glimpses of imploring
rose, lying in a room bare except for five

books, about what is called 'death'—
a vogue, a blossoming, a failure, a few
stars. It was a sad year, we seem to be
going on with the old threads

or it looks threadable by slight
fingers. Did I call him to me,
had he come too near, he is waiting
by the icy runway, my hand is wonderfully
surprised, my hand is in his hand
and is my contact with Amen.

It is my lifeblend to write towards
a lessness; I should daydream
in the night as I used to. Then the night
is cut in half as, afterwards, he had walked
into me. I have my litany, my minute
knowledge of sleepless angels.

Mirror for Eight Voices

The voice of my father entered my head
though the door had disappeared long ago.
The dew of his grave will heal every trouble of weather.

Sometimes a day is a stepmother, sometimes a mother.
The evangelic morning separates dream from ghost:
a ghost that felt life-sized, leaps up into the bell.

Pain-giver dawn and the turned-up sky reworking
the whispers, tugging a thread in an old tapestry,
a prayer retreat to ease the afterlife of her mother.

Her soul disrobing, like a silver bowl collecting snow,
a blue martyrdom which wasn't able to make the wind
divide the flower from itself, though various levels of flower exist.

The cherry, revisited by blossoms, madly blooming,
writes in so unmeant a style, an almost verbal vanishing.
The hedges grow leggy and tall, forlorn, undisciplined

hedges like these. The world inside the window, a world
without faiths, is an ice-church relieved only by the arm
of the chair, the morbidly gold cellar light of the unshaded

swaying lights, to which the vagueness of this angel
returns sadly. I tended to speak in a spiritually laden
language, a richer dust for the moon's interpretation.

The eyes of the scornful and graceless seraphim felt
heavy on me, in a funnel of shadow, the moment when
the shadows line up. In their cruel radiance I set out

looking for young black me. We live in a city within
a city; they have theirs and we have ours. In the lily-
white suburbs black smudges spread upwards in the shape

of tombstones, buildings cluster together as if they were toxic.
It's like going back through death, line and stain
of the lessness to come, the endless limbs of the sentence.

One swooning, long, festal, baby's dress, of the most frail muslin,
hand-sewn in painfully laboured small stitchings, folded, not pressed.
A mirror carried along a road, feeling for rings on their fingers.

Self-portrait with Large Collar

The shade lane leads to the white shell path
where the composer is buried directly behind the piano.
The light beyond touches it, the soft whites of the room,
but the master scent that I discern is that of death.

So I shall suggest that you cling a lesser time to the world
of humans, for this garden with this dragonfly table is the last.
The lightning undresses the wide expanse of mauve sand
in the final shutdown of some piece of life, as we have known it to be.

And I become more interested in the perfection of skeletons,
prisoners of ivy, less truly violated, though the peaceful birds
are free to come and go. I won't have this God, he is no use to me,
his voice is already threadbare, though we see the makings of a throat

in something, surrounded by something, in a decaying chapel.
Is he burning a rose, or holding what may be a lamp, or crown?
The words are hand-sewn, embroidered, cut into wood, breathed,
or stirred in water. Unlaboured images, cradled in their voluminous

turn of the century clothes. They tie their skirts to produce
complex patterns of folds, they step forward, further agitating the cloth,
rustling the pearl trimmings. My silken Adam and Eve,
creatures of infernal spring, where I sewed my mind

with a pin shaped like a swallow, in a tedious sampler
is like a book that has spent time in the sea. When you
wrote that line of glass, or blurred windows, I wanted
to be near water, or any naked colour, though I forget

what yellow means. I turned upon that commonplace
angel with her bleached and frighted face,
within the squalid kitchen, the honest tablecloths.
Tomorrow I'll go and look for nettles.

Self-portrait with Jewish Passport

Oceans open and close in the moonlights.
Amber chains are attached to the tip of his tongue,
a close up of the dappled underside
of a sea star's tonic immobility.

Its internal wave is large enough
to hold an atmosphere. The sun
sailing to nowhere, on the sky sewn
on to the world, can pull some great

truth out of an ocean, can cut
the ultimate tether, tangible, aged,
authentic. The idea that the dead
lie in numbered rooms that are trying

to wrap themselves up, a Paradise
more bloody than a battlefield.
Why were we never so happy, so free,
as under the occupation? What peace

(and here I am talking about inner
peace)—the city was prised open
so as not to injure a sentence,
I lost myself in that city more

than twenty years ago. Memories
peer from the shelf, pain without
aboutness, but still with compulsion,
the heart of is and isn't.

The heart that can be felt
is not the unchanging heart, is
a horizon change. Some connections
get pruned away by the soul of rain.

In the strangely simple present
the city itself was losing sanity,
its nerves fraying, its love depleted,
its patience spent self-bleeding.

The camera follows in the path
of the gun, the path paths itself
into icy pined undeath, a spinal
landscape bearing near and far names

of the Mass Path, the Night Field, Shed
Field, House Field, Field Under the House,
Night Island, Sea Shepherd.
Walking on dry rivers, dry valleys,

he measures the field with his thought,
the passion of the window, its power
of cloud. The finite moon reading,
it doesn't try to be full.

Its spirit blushes like the clay,
one will die, one will live.
Life may be all there is,
or the shake of new life, the future

child, the voice-to-be, an angel-
animal darking you out, field
rose, yellow archangel, roseroot,
frost hollows, personification of winter.

In the dry summer of 1950
I became accustomed to seeing the field,
promising the eye a natural step.
We no longer see it well.

When I drive by the field
what I see is different from what I imagine,
the makings of an answer
where I ask all night.

The field retained our shapes,
sometimes softened by snow. I am reminded
every year of these workings
of the field, its gypsiness.

Its colours varied with the time of day,
a piece of yellow taffeta to be worn
above the heart and blend so well
with the dead leaves.

A flowing curtain, a ruffled tablecloth,
a glass bed with glass sheets,
brown cedar parlour
in a sea of claret and blue,

an otherwise uninvited black,
the jade snow and sky-view factor
of the flat cemetery. The air
entrapped in the ice-core

of the light-demanding tree
forced it into the city
which might have been a text
that no one would ever read.

From where we're sitting
on the shoulders of Ireland
the towering stack of pallets
for the bonfire has grown significantly in size.

(The urge to festivalize.)
This braille has vanished,
this pixillated kiss, the rib-like shadows
clogging the low-lit corridors of The Maze.

For such a word is badly wanted
like the soundwalk I took
with a woman angel, to lift these sounds
found in the English of my mind.

Our friendship might have skated
but something will die in me which is meant
to be immortal, unless I go back, do nothing
but breathe, above the city dust line.

1

Our windows are holding their breath
at the price of light; my wraparound
window is lifting me out of the slanting
room wherein I slept.

Lame Sappho, with purple breastbows,
you don't feel the years, you feel
the decades, the endless recycling
of meaning, the everyday memoryscapes.

This once all-conquering impure,
she is quite undone; she may possibly
come about again but she must not
to the opera on a day of miscarriage.

My silver leg has tripped against a star.
The sea is just the two shades eyelash
of the river's river writing. The stars
are entered by familiar eyeshine,

neon-blue looks and every form of way.
Sunlight filters through an angel's skirt

like the mountain's wartime shadows
from the cameras dug into its face.

2

We are too prey to the stop and frisk
laws, the lemonpeel angelfish, the baffling
swallow, even the high fantastical
Duchess of Newcastle in her lightful house.

The skybreak was doubled from the outside
to almost nothingness. We tried to give
this house memories, of the black cloud marks,
the radiant or damp heaven, its untethered thereless.

The unbidden thought is from the dead,
from their newly minted boundaries
when I may shape the dark to a distant
dearness in the hill of my childhood.

Fallen leaves interleave, leaving these closures
ajar. The unshared beauty of the door
between your shoulders is like the skin of caves,
the return that drags us away.

As different as movement and daydream,
rain bathing the roses, bees undercover,

the metropolis is obsolete—ask the army,
ask the computer in a plague of echoes.

It is a world without lines for later-born
Theresas, over the fields of the sea,
in the days of sometime. The past returns
unbeckoned, smooth quick sliding after week.

3

The planet rolls eager into winter,
taunting summer for its lateness,
waking the angels beyond time fallen
on the time floor, spring after spring.

The maternal angel felt herself
covered by a fine veil of steel
and nine chains to the moon
holding busloads of angel luggage.

The gestures which you said you didn't have
are a costly something or nothing,
still another thing filled with the intent
to be lost, like the verb 'to north'.

The sky and its soul of rare
and commonplace flowers has even now

that care. She feels she has become
illegible, letting a question furrow deeper:

what is a friend in the feminine
and who in the feminine is her friend?
I put my story on hold, life never being
as it is, it has to be here

for the pearl to take shape, the black
angel that means in her its first white
flight. The crossed lips of the becoming
angel bring an unsolicited vision

of all actual angels, of the many
angels produced in outright dreams,
God's secret agents,
immune to the night,

the yellowish six-winged angel
and the two-headed angel of parking
with its immense collar of clouds
hinged to an autumn season.

Black Angel

The sea is speckled with meagre sunlight
like sequins torn from the mask of the moon,
a planet of faces. The land is as close
as the organs inside us; the language is thinning

in the ribbons of the motorway. On summer
afternoons separated by decades we see
the fracture, flexure, contraction of the earth
as a ghost that cannot die enough, the thaw

of all those vanities. Psychopharmacologically
stabilized, in a techno-angelic transfiguration,
a cosmo-political slowing down, I poison
the unshoreline in bitter nutmeg and wine.

Black Garden

Each cloud is fully rammed
into the moodily lit cathedral
but the low sky does not open
so our undelivered letter is dead.

The graves are marked with clean
silk flowers for the end of summer.
The trees are quiet as a rusty eye
depicting the hum of rivers.

What kind of traces have I left
to pick out a casket-like carpet
at the back of the pews? Voice of a
wisteria vine talking from the graveyard.

It was the last nice street before
the town fell. They are not quite ghosts,
just dust, gathering shapes, caressing
the movement of time, the detail of the daily.

Down to the feeling of cloth
from the fleshless statue-person,
with a glove the schoolgirl sweeps away
snow from Meredith's grave, weather for winter weather.

Badly scarred but regrowing trees
hold boulders in their peasant roots.
The woman holds her rosary, with the end of her mouth,
without lips, and stares at the television.

The Moondial

They avoid providing their fingerprints by burning their fingers.

Cups of nighttime water
are all that lifts easily
to another's lips. My ever-giving body
must have self-lit from any red
interruption to the grey they offer.

The city seems to fall into pieces,
steered into a sliding cloud, goes rib
to rib, leans in to run the warning
out of my body where many
wintry things keep adding up.

At least I recognized the yellow thought,
caresses of an arm in days gone by,
or some Februaries that match,
geranium kiss inside the rain.
The flags are frozen, don't move in wind;

they carry no sentiment. Flowers freeze
in liquid air and thick lake-effect snow.
For nineteen days I do the candles

to uncertain saints (why are saints'
feet silver?). The brown garden,

fatal flower garden, stores a threadbare rose
of pressed blue until the bone blinks through,
until the ceasefire ceases. A sky not bare
of leather stars stands over their heads
in the hunched chapels. Clearly for them

everything had become words. When she read
her sibling's diary, those deserving mother/daughter
dreams (time can be shared), the blood had begun
like the morning. Cleaning buildings
late at night makes her bleed slowly;
you are that below river wave.

The Snowfall Room

The mesmerizing weather
has a very rich yellowing
like the sky over Verdun
and Railway Hollow Wood.

Feet over leaves in the thin
remnant of air
try to account
for the fallen leaves

or what happened
to our promised moon—
five great dyings
blurring their stars together.

The change of a certain
sound makes the star
more and more
peachlike, the earth

would find itself
inside a star,
the heart of a star.
The starlanes littered

with the eyes of stars,
but fewer blue-white
stars. Archaic sparrows
probe the crowded starfields

of the flying angel
painter, whose musical
salvation is how to find
the North, to touch her leaves.

The Chrysanthemum Hour

In spite of all one is a northerner at heart.

Before there were centuries there were
long drawn-out sunsets watching
the egg-shaped moonpath cutting down
the stairway.

Her close wool, her good bone, her love
for her own private Lucifer, prised away
daylight, the percentage of deaths shrinks
in its socket of ice.

This winter is not a success, this is
a summer gone wrong, the autumn sky
is gilded and bare, like an answered
prayer.

There is more river in you than shoreland.
Breathe on it and it scatters like a spirit
in a coat, a close-sheared meadow,
a very old angel, so they say,

but so much younger than we. In the calm
of this first week of Lent I have sinful dreams.

More than kin was at stake, something sunk
in something else.

The setting sun holds out its heavy wings,
their patches of imperfect blue. My sense
of smell inhabited some space
behind my eyes,

lodged in my stomach, nurturing those
almost finished feelings. The autumn
I have is the autumn I lost, as if the autumn
were beginning in us

rather than in the world. When the wind
allows it autumn will take everything,
half-slept interludes always in the room
next door.

In the dull silence of my strangely hollow
body my sight is fringed by a state
of perpetually restored virginity, false
whiteness of the moon.

If I think the moonlight with my feelings
a mist crouches in the sky, stirring up cold
ashes, until all at once the silence stopped,
surly beaks of gondolas.

Why did you not kneel down at the Sanctus,
your monthly roses like a row of cypresses
swarming up to the house, defeated rain
of a dead summer?

You thought yourself a dark and shapeless
Madonna with over-delicate hands. Perhaps
only in Proserpina's bed would I sleep
well, the place

where I bury my best bones, the dead yellow
fields of myself. Single leaves as they fall
rest in bejewelled silver coffins; you pin
the sun to your breast.

So the moon with that distinct blue
bruise on its face, is the forgiveness of the stranger
who by chance, brought you into the world.
Are we the same people?

A Particular Friendship

Milkfish-sunbear-clouded leopard-
seawasp—his English was always at its worst
in the mornings or when he was at pains
to shed his Englishness:

you have some subtle thought and it
comes out as a piece of broken bottle.
Beginning to hear the words as voices,
though they spoke then without voices,

he began to dream he was back in London
during the Blitz, had arrived without an overcoat
as though it were a recent hurt,
in Image-town, the beautiful,

where they rang the bells backwards.
He had been looking for the perfect city,
maybe it begins with W
in his first made-up language.

To be fair to his younger self
it is something to do with the rain the day
before, when you rekiss kisses,
white road without cars, written

in Joyce Esperanto or macaronic
with the pencil the hospital allowed.
He told the headmaster he didn't care
for Plato, and read books few others

had heard of (most of his favourites were
on the Index). He wore a navy-blue turtle-
neck sweater, spent money on silk ties
he wondered if he would ever wear—

they were after all in the best of taste.
He wore a soft felt hat which he threw
like a frisbee, a gold watch chain
on which he had no watch.

Lone operator, she suspected him
of being a spy for the other side,
that he took up spying for sport—
she prayed for him when nobody else did.

One movie he saw through four times,
smoking his *Craven 'A'* or *Players N°. 3*
downing a concoction called *Vimto*
or *Harvey's Shooting Sherry.*

He kept his lips tight shut when others
were praying in the chapel but hung about
thinking of the white monks in the novel:
there were times when he wondered

if only names made sense—the stations
on the railway, a catalogue of advertising
slogans, the names of the ships that sailed
to Troy—the name of every girl

he had thought himself in love with.
He would have liked the shared silence
and protection of an older woman.
(His Aunt Maud died that November.)

Cold but passionate, he spent his evenings
in one pub or another, as if he were doubled
up over an oar the whole time, enjoying
the craziness of the place, though he says

nothing about the huge Peace March, or Hunger
March, he talked of Reds in an ill-defined way.
He would sign a petition and probably picketed,
sold some pamphlets and made some kind of speech

in the big classroom during the strike.
Editor of the yearbook, he was good
at drawing footballers, and could do imitations
of Baby Face Nelson. First and last,

a literary youth, he walked explosively
with verse as in a trance both merry and sober;
poet of the rain, he wrote of the inkpot
and of the pen he was using for whatever warm

book, fingers together in a pear shape.
A cartoonist's picture of an Irishman,
moonfaced, caustic, and witty,
he had young eyes, one of the best glances

upwards waiting in the dismal bus station.
Like something of a dream-return
of torn theatre tickets, he came in and out
of view at times of his own choosing,

mouth still burning from the night before.
For him the Mass was a ballet, still
its sermon made him sore, two flushes
of new leaves on the daylilies in the spartan

parlour could find his leaving
believable, very believing unbeliever.

Awakening Day

Each day has so much to say, one does not dare
to say anything about it oneself.
Sometimes the bus route is the map,
and none of the weather really belongs.

These wild fluctuations, blight and ruin,
two versions of winter, errands to kill the day;
leaves fall later in weather's increasing absence
despite the multiple, divergent weathers.

A face-palm moment reconciles your soul
to its new garment, the aura of undying
doesn't continue to turn. It was the fourth day
of rain, on the days which is most of them.

As to the destination of the munitions,
well, it was obvious. Ravenous dead
around the only exit, classic fields
streamlining the spirit, running between streams.

A site of endlessness, the dot-com bubble.
It could, this time, really fall
into the Sun, whose eruptions prevent
unrecognizable seasons.